PASSION FRUIT

BY DIOR CLARKE
AND STEPH MARTIN

Published April 2025 by Team Angelica Publishing,
an imprint of Angelica Entertainments Ltd

Team Angelica Publishing
51 Coningham Road
London W12 8BS

TEAM
ANGELICA

www.teamangelica.com

A CIP catalogue record for this book is available from
the British Library

ISBN 978-1-7397739-5-3

Cover photograph by Rikki Beadle-Blair
Perry's rap by Big Zeeko; reproduced with permission

CREDITS:

Writers: Dior Clarke & Steph Martin
Director/designer: Rikki Beadle-Blair
Produced by: Loquaciously Unfiltered Productions, in co-production with Barbican Centre and Cambridge Junction

Cast:
Troy Alexander
Selina Armoudon
Ashley Byam
Dior Clarke

Movement direction: Kane Husbands of The Pappy Show
Lighting design: Rori Endersby
Sound design: Kayode Gomez
Stage Manager: Crystal Gayle

PRODUCTION NOTE:

This extensively reworked and rewritten version of *Passion Fruit* was first performed at the Barbican Centre and Cambridge Junction, April-May 2025.

WITH THANKS TO:

David Byrne and New Diorama, Kane Husbands and The Pappy Show, Reece McMahon, Jahmila Heath, Malachi Giscombe, David Shopland, Katie Pesskin, Jessica Monaghan and the Seven Dials Playhouse. Bertie Watkins and COLAB, Toni Racklin, Liz Eddy and the Barbican Centre team, Matt Burman and Cambridge Junction.

PRODUCTION HISTORY:

Passion Fruit was commissioned and developed by New Diorama Theatre in association with The Pappy Show, and was first performed at New Diorama Theatre in March 2022 with the following team:

Director: Melina Namdar
Dramaturg: Rikki Beadle-Blair
Design: Sandra Falase
Sound Design: Kayode Gomez
Lighting Design: Martha Godfrey
Stage Manager: Crystal Gayle
Movement Director: Kane Husbands
Associate Movement Director: Mateus Daniel
Cast: Dior Clarke, Charlotte Gosling and Hayden Mampasi

*

INTRODUCTION
by Rikki Beadle-Blair

Hosting the main stage of UK Black Pride is a privilege that no little gay boy growing up on the streets of Bermondsey in the '60s and '70s could ever have dreamed of. Can you imagine the homophobia and the racism back then? Sometimes casual, affectionate even, and sometimes terrifyingly violent, it was a minefield. You had to watch every step. It was hard to imagine that anyone who attracted such savage energy could survive. But here we were. On a huge stage in a huge park overflowing with thousands of joyous revellers, black, brown, tan and white, of all sexualities and gender expressions, celebrating black queerness in the summer sun.

And there at the front of the crowd was a slender, doe-eyed teenage beauty, waving, whooping and dancing like a diva. I broke the rules and invited the beauty and his friends to climb the barrier, and persuaded security to let them come up and show off their Jamaican dancehall moves. Splits, twerking, wining their waists and celebrating their carefree youth and unashamed beauty. Wow. We had all come so far.

Time to introduce the next main stage performer. I thew my arms open to the dancing diva-ette and thanked him for his incandescence. He threw himself at me and threw his arms around me and cried out, 'We're gonna work together one day!'

And, ten years later, here we are. Working on Dior's first play, *Passion Fruit*. And what a play. The energy, the passion, the wit and confusion of growing up in a world that is so much gayer, blacker and more working class and femme than it thinks it is. Fighting for visibility. For meaning. For balance. For self-love. Fighting for survival. Survival of the spirit.

Everything that Dior and his amazing co-writer Steph have observed, experienced, channelled and expressed in this rumbustious and defiantly elegant work of art speaks to me and for me. And when they see or hear about it, or feel its ripple effect, trust me, all the kids out there, walking the mean streets, killing fields and suffocating suburbs will some-how know that there they are, being spoken up for by this brilliant play. It's what James Baldwin, Tennessee Williams and Sylvester were for me. A dream catapult I didn't know I was dreaming of and praying for. Every possibility seemed so impossible. And yet. Here we are. And here you are.

FROM THE WRITERS #1: Dior Clarke

I remember being aged ten, staring up at the stars painted on my bedroom ceiling at night, asking God to help me make my mum, bros, sis, grandparents, aunties and cousins proud. To help me break generational curses. To find the strength to live in my full, unapologetic truth and conquer my dreams. To ingrain in the world that no matter who you are or where you're from, you can achieve anything if a working class Gay Black Jamaican British-born boy from North London Hornsey could.

After a few years of highs and lows navigating myself through the arts world I loved so much but rarely saw people like me existing in, having idols such as Rikki-Beadle-Blair, John Gordon, Tyler Perry, Lee Daniels, Billy Porter, Patrik-Ian Polk, Ryan Murphy, Russell T Davies and Michaela Cole producing stories I felt seen in, I decided it was my time to tell a story only I could. In 2018 I co-wrote, directed and acted in a Sky Arts 10-minute short film, *Batty Boy*, a semi-autobiographical and uncompromising take on black gay culture unmasked, set against homophobia and dancehall music.

I knew there was so much more of the world of the story to share.

'Five years ago, I didn't really believe there were other black gay people out there – if I'd seen a film like this back then, it would have reassured me that I wasn't alone, and perhaps it wouldn't have taken me as long to realise who I was.'

It was perfect timing when the beautiful and talented Steph Martin, my writing wife, reached out to me to collaborate, after meeting in a bar and watching *Batty Boy*. How romantic! We got to work and *Passion Fruit* was cultivated; a story inspired by my life and things I have seen, sprinkled with Steph's magic.

In 2021 *Passion Fruit* hit the Glory, achieving sold-out previews and rapturous audience responses. In 2022 it had its sold-out world premier run at The New Diorama, directed by the fab Melina Namdar and gaining five-star reviews, two

Black British Theatre Award wins (out of five nominations), and two Off West End nominations – for best movement and ensemble.

Now here we come, Barbican and Cambridge Junction! The new Beyoncé elevation of *Passion Fruit*, directed by the GOAT Rikki-Beadle Blair and produced by my production company Loquaciously Unfiltered, an urban 'hood' narrative told for the first time from a queer perspective on these stages. How essential it is to have achieved this! As 'Black Lives Matter' even more now than ever, *Passion Fruit* is a story that is urgently needed, as it asks the question, 'Do Black LGBTQ+ Lives matter yet?!'

Homophobia is rife in the black community and is a shameful, discriminatory and poisonous subject that is rarely spoken about. My people are still losing their lives.

Passion Fruit will educate on this subject and give young black LGBTQ+, and LGBTQ* people in general, a voice! *Passion Fruit* will give them the confidence to say, 'Yes, I do exist and what!' Based on the majority of the media it would be easy to believe they *don't* exist. But over the years of being seasoned I've realised that fluidity is the majority. Saying that, my mission is not anymore to reverse the hate, but to dedicate my art to the ones who appreciate and need it!

I've learnt no matter what, LOVE YOURSELF!

I know it's cliché but trust me, you have to find your way – which will forever change every day, but that's life. Surround yourself by people who love you and lift you. Respect your worth and know you're enough, like my OG Gailen Young taught me.

Own your downfalls, your flaws, and let them blossom into your superpowers.

Treat and love people the way you yearn to be treated.

I wanna thank the number one woman in my life: my mum, aka Melanie Clarke, for unconditionally being a Black

British-born Jamaican women who accepts me regardless of culture norms and values, my grandma Gloria Clarke, and my siblings Paige, Tye and Shanny Loo. My cousin Sharday Clarke, who showed me the ropes.

My besties Maekeesha Fuller, who began and is still on the journey with me, and Natalie Seals, who never gives up on me.

All the mainstream institutions and people who allowed me to be seen: London School of Dramatic Arts, National Youth Theatre, Creative England, Sky Arts, ALRA, The Glory, New Diorama, Byron's Management, Nicola Bolton, Jess Jones and Carey Dodds. Ms Audra Daws Knowles, Ms Stables, Jake Taylour, Samantha Robinsons, Judy Brown, Samuel Evans, Carolina Gimametta.

THIS ONE'S FOR THE CULTURE!
THIS ONE'S FOR MY FAMILY!
RIP SHAHI SURGEON-HOLDER, GRANDMA WALLACE,
LOLISA TAYLOR AND JOSEPH WHITTER.
GOOD BETTER BEST, NEVER LET IT REST UNTIL YOUR
GOOD IS BETTER AND YOUR BETTER IS BEST.
GOD DON'T SLEEP!

FROM THE WRITERS #2: Steph Martin

Dior and I met in a bar just over 10 years ago, two strangers with nothing to connect them. But a connection was forged, a spark was lit. We were laughing, energising and celebrating each other from day one. Fast forward to today and we're 5 years into a writing partnership and collaboration. Our stories are almost always about self-discovery, self-love, self-doubt, self-determination, love found, love lost and found again, ambition, mistakes, friendship, motherhood, brotherhood and family. A reflection of the London of today, a place of energy, possibility and a whole range of challenges, personal and political to overcome.

Dedication: For Mum, Dad and Sam who make it all possible; and for my two sons – may you love stories and people as much as I do.

CLARKE/MARTIN

PASSION FRUIT

Characters:

ROMEO – Jamaican-British, from childhood-adulthood
PERRY – Jamaican-British, from childhood-adulthood
MUM – Jamaican-British, 30s-40s
DAD – Jamaican-British, 40s
VIV – Jamaican-British, 40s
AARON – Black British, from childhood-adulthood
RIZZLA – Black British, teenager
EVE – Black British, teenager
GRANDMA – Jamaican, 70s
JERMAINE – Jamaican, 40s
SAMI – Black British, late 20s
PANELLIST 1, White British, 50s
PANELLIST 2, White British, 50s

*Other characters include: partygoers, club DJs, chem sex
hosts, drama school auditionees.*

Setting:

London, from 1998 to the present.

ACT ONE

Music plays: 'Bootilicious' – Destiny's Child. Lights up on Romeo, doing the most, dancing like his life depends on it.

The music scratches.

Romeo: Mum… I'm gay.

A beat.

Romeo greets the audience with warmth and humour.

Romeo: Surprise!

Well, I'm glad that's over and done with. This ain't a coming out story. This is a love story. A self-love story. It's like RuPaul says: 'If you can't love yourself…'

Romeo encourages the audience to join him in saying, 'how the hell are you gonna love somebody else?!'

Romeo: It's 1998 on the Lightfoot Estate, North London. I'm five years old, with my big brother Perry, and Mum's painting our nails.

Mum: *(Sighs)* This is the last time I'm doing this.

Romeo/Perry: Whyyy?

Mum: Because you're boys not girls.

Romeo: Why's it only for girls?

Mum: It just is. Men don't paint their nails.

Perry: I don't want it then. I'm not a girl, take it off.

Romeo: Why though?

Mum: That's just the way it is.

Romeo: But, why?

2

Perry: Mum!

Mum: For God's sake, will you just 'llow me, nuh? Romeo, stop acting like such a bitch. Have you got a pussy?

Romeo is hurt. Mum notices and immediately softens.

Mum: You know Mummy just wants you to be safe. I don't want no one to mess with mi baby. Come dance wid Mummy. Perry, you too.

'Come Fly with Me' (feat. Sizzla) – Foxy Brown plays. Mum and Romeo dance together, bussing their best wine, girl band style – in perfect, practised unison. Perry joins in begrudgingly, pretending not to enjoy himself.

Dad: Take that off, now!

Mum, Romeo and Perry freeze in their tracks. They know what Dad's anger means.

Dad: And turn off that atrocious music!

Mum: Perry, Romeo, go to your room.

Romeo: *(To audience)* Me and Perry are hiding in our bedroom in the dark, listening to the sounds of violence through the wall.

Romeo: Perry, you go and look.

Perry: No, you go.

Romeo: You go, you're older.

Perry: It's your turn.

Romeo: If you go, I'll let you choose all the games for the next week.

Perry: Nah.

Romeo: Okay, the whole month.

Perry: No.

Romeo: You're so annoying. Such a pussy.

Perry: You're the pussy! Only pussies like getting their nails done like a girl.

Romeo: Shut your mouth and go and see if Mum's okay, please!

A beat.

Perry: I hate dad.

Romeo: You can't say that.

Perry: It's true. I wish he was dead, I wish he got hit by a car and had a heart attack and dropped down dead.

Romeo: Don't say that!

A beat.

Perry: I'm scared.

Romeo: Let's play stories.

Perry: You always want to play stories, it's boring.

Romeo: I've got a sick one in my head and you can be the main character.

Dad: Romeo, Perry downstairs. Now.

Perry: I ain't going.

Perry is resolute. Romeo moves to the kitchen.

Romeo: *(To audience)* Mum's sitting with her back to me, silent. I sneak a look at her face, it's dotted with blood, like nails have been dragged down it.

4

Dad: What did you learn in school today? What happened in 1066? Come on, Romeo.

Romeo: Battle of Hastings, innit.

Dad: Good boy. But it ain't innit, it's 'isn't it', you get me? Speak proper English. None of that slang.

Romeo: Yes, Dad.

Dad: See that's why you're my little king. You're different from them ragamuffins round ya suh, you are better than them. Education is key, distance yourself from all of that nastiness. We're better than your mother's people dem, dutty immigrants. I want you to stay away from them black thug children, play with the white children from nice houses. Work hard. Mek your father proud.

Romeo: Yes, Dad.

Dad turns on Mum.

Dad: You hear that? My boys are going to be big men. Well-groomed, well-educated. Class. Not like you. You're a low and classless embarrassment with your nasty reggae music, and you know that, don't you, Marina?

Mum: Yeah.

Dad: Yeah, what?

Mum: Yeah, I know that.

Dad: Speak up. You know what?

Mum: I know I'm dumb.

Dad: You're pathetic.

Mum: I know.

Dad: No one else would put up with you.

Mum: I know.

Dad: Look at you, look at what I have to deal with!

Romeo: *(To audience)* I struggle to remember this. I feel like I'm making it all up.

Dad continues to taunt Mum.

Dad: You silly, nasty, dirty, uneducated little sket. You've done nothing, you've got nothing, you are nothing. You are wotless. How the hell would you ever survive without me?

Romeo: *(To audience)* But she does.

Mum: *(Barely audible)* Get out.

Dad: What did you say?

Mum: *(Growing in confidence)* I said. Get out. Putting your hands on me and my babies. Then they gotta watch and hear you beating the shit out of me. NO MORE. I'm done. We're done. Get the fuck out. Come out!

Romeo: *(To audience)* Police arrive to remove him from our home. I watch from the front room window as they take him away, down the path.

Music plays, soft and tender. Mum dances, slow, in her own world. Romeo and Perry watch as if through the bannisters.

Romeo: *(To audience)* That night Mum lights a spliff and turns the music up. To me she is the number one dance-hall queen. I wanna wine my waist like her, I wanna dip like her but boys don't wine their waists, boys don't dip.

*****

Auntie Viv comes round and they party all night long. The

music and mood change from reflective and soothing to celebration and rave. Beenie Man – 'Dancehall Queen' plays. Mum and Viv dance together energetically and fully.

Viv: Man-them is all the same. All of dem is dogs! Just some are well trained. Mi telling you, Marina, they're only good for one ting, so you need fi know how fi train dem. Use them for what you want and that's it, don't even let them stay the night, boot dem out and mek them go about their business and rest your head peace. Stress free, my gal.

Mum: *(Laughing)* Woiiiiiiiiiiiii you give mi joke!

Viv: Mi telling you, them can't help it, it's inna dem blood. Dutty waste men. Mi can't bother with dem fuckery. At home I have mi dog, mi good good vibrator and mi go a gym – that's enough for me.

Mum: Oh, lord, Viv, you ain't easy.

Viv: Use dem, mek dem take you out someplace nice. Have one fi the light bill, one fi the phone bill, one fi the rent, one fi shopping and one for extras. PAY DOWN PON IT! You gotta get out dating, my gyal!

Mum: Oh no, not yet, Viv. Man is di last ting pon mi mind.

Viv: Time for some fresh romance, some fun, now that bastard scrub is gone.

Mum: Yeah... but I ain't ready!

Viv: You're right. No need to rush. That is some premium pussy you have down there.

Mum: Million dollar pum-pum.

Viv: Pum-pum million dollar! Not just for any old bruck-down man.

They toast and find themselves very amusing.

Mum and Viv: Premium pussy.

Romeo: *(To audience)* What they talking about a pussy for? We don't have a cat.

Mum, are we getting a cat?!

Mum beckons to Perry and Romeo.

Mum: Now listen, you two, promise me that you won't let no one stop you from doing what you want. People are gonna try and control and mould you into what they want you to be. People are always gonna judge you and chat shit about you. My boys are better than that. Promise me?

Romeo and Perry: Promise.

Mum: I have big dreams for you two. Repeat after me. 'I am a strong black man.'

Romeo and Perry: *(Begrudgingly)* I am a strong black man.

Mum: I am a strong, vulnerable black man.

Perry: Vulnerable?! Nah.

Romeo: This is stupid.

Perry: I'm not weak!

Mum: Say it. I am a strong, vulnerable, talented, black man.

Perry: I'm not saying it!

Mum clips Perry round the ear.

Mum: *(Very stern)* Say it.

Mum's telling off prompts Romeo and Perry to follow her lead.

Romeo and Perry: I am a strong, vulnerable, talented black man.

'Forward' - Lethal Bizzle plays, building in volume. Romeo is trying 'butch roadman' poses in his bedroom mirror, making sure his cap is on at the correct angle. The company join him and display teenage boy masculinity.

Romeo: *(To audience)* I'm 13 now and everyone's changing. All the boys at school are talking about mashing up the pum-pum.

Rizzla: Big man ting. Last night, I was getting the sloppiest head,

Perry: Mine had the biggest batty, she had a fat punani.

Rizzla: So what you sayin' Romeo, what happened with you and that peng ting the other night?

Perry: Romeo's always got bare gyal around him, he's a proper gyalist.

Romeo: You don' know, my G. I gotta keep my runnings a secret though, not cock block myself, like you likkle immature dickheads.
(To audience) My brother is the one I must impress. He's a leader. No one messed with him.

Perry: *(The sort of wisdom people find when they're stoned)* I'm telling you, man, reptiles are in the government, they ARE the government, like all the global billionaires are reptiles and they are controlling the world's media. Queen Lizzie is Queen Lizard, it's literally in her name, real talk, I'm telling you this freemason ting is REAL.

Rizzla: Deeeeeeep!!!

Perry: I'm the enlightened one, innit. My mind is open to the truth and therefore the truth has come to me. It's all on YouTube, plain to see.

Rizzla: Is it? Skeen, I'll have to check it out.

Perry: You lot need to take the time to educate yourself.

Romeo: *(To audience)* After school the boys watch porn together. The DVD goes in the PS2 and everyone unzips, their eyes fixed on the gyal dem on the screen. I try and focus. 'Boobs boobs boobs', forget Perry stroking over here, don't watch Rizzla bussin' a nut over there. 'Boobs'. 'Punani'. 'Vagina'.

Rizzla: Listen yeah. Who has the biggest dick? Anyone got a ruler?

Romeo turns to a male audience member.

Romeo: Did you used to do that with your mates?

Romeo waits for the audience member to respond.

Romeo: I'll take that as a yes.

I think I'm getting away with it but the boys are always hassling me, pointing out the cracks in my 'masculinity'.

Perry: Bro, you need to fix up the way you flex, people are talking. They say you walk like a gyal, you speak like a gyal.

Rizzla: *(To audience)* That's cause man's gay, innit.

Romeo is used to these taunts and is determined not to let on. He plays the role of the homophobic teenage boy he thinks he needs to be.

Romeo: Shut up, I'm just in touch with my feminine side, innit, stop chatting shit.

Rizzla: Why you always hanging with the gyaldem, Romeo?

Perry: Because he like gyals, he's beating up pum-pum after pum-pum. Where's your gyal, pussy'ole?

Rizzla: Your brother's the one who got a pussy'ole!

Romeo kisses his teeth.

Perry: Fuck you, neek. His name's literally Romeo, are you mad?

Romeo: Yeah, show me your gyal, chi chi man! You're the one that likes getting your back bruck off. I've got pussy in north, west, south and east, I got pussy in outer space, I got pussy that's got one foot in the grave. But the biggest pussyhole I know is you, batty man. You like it up your raas, you dirty diseased faggot poof.

Perry: Ohhhhhhh, Rizzla's a batty man!!

Romeo: Can you imagine putting your dick in a bum? That shit's nasty, fam.

Rizzla: I aint gay, fam. You're the batty boy, it's bait.

Perry: Are you gonna have that, Romeo?

Romeo: Keep pushing me. Keep pushing me.

Rizzla: Gay, Gay, Gay, Gay, Gay –

Romeo: Carry on –

Rizzla: You gay boy, you batty bwoy bruv!

Romeo finally gives in and begins to fight Rizzla. His embarrassment, fear, shame and anger take over. They fight.

Perry steps in to protect Romeo, separating him and Rizzla.

Perry: Enough! Relax, relax.

Rizzla: Chill, bro, chill. I was just playing.

Perry: 'Llow it, both of you. We need to focus. Tonight is gonna be the perfect opportunity to release our diss track back to the Wood Green boys. There's gonna be bare smoke, bare drink, bare gyals and all the Hornsey Grey Gang will be there.

Romeo: *(To audience)* We arrive at the party that night, ready to rule and shut it down.

Music plays: 'Hot Fuck' – Mr Vegas. The company fill the space to show us the hood party. Movement sequence to convey the thrill, fun and them uniting as one: teenage boys experiencing friendship, freedom and possibility.

Romeo: *(To audience)* The bass of the music vibrates, courses through my body. I feel it in my chest, in my heart, in each of my organs. The crowd moves together like a flame, like everything could explode at any moment.

You feel it too, yeah? I know you do. You remember what it feels like to be young.

Romeo loses himself in the music.

DJ: This next tune is for all the Real Tuggz in the building. No man to man ting round here. Wi waan bunn out all dutty Sodomite Batty Bwoi business. No man to man ting!

Crowd: No man to man ting!

A homophobic track blast through the speaker.

The energy of the rave shifts. The crowd begins singing and chanting along to the violent, homophobic lyrics.

Romeo acknowledges it. Everything slows down. The music

echoes and the bodies begin to decline as we see him battle within himself.

Romeo: *(To audience)* Inside, I'm rooted to the ground. The bass begins to rip through my insides. Is this unity? Or is this rejection? I ain't a batty man, I've never been with a boy. Do I walk out or do I dance? I love this bass, I love my culture, this is who I am, this is where I'm from.

Fuck it, let's dance.

The music suddenly rushes in and we crash back into reality. Romeo dances more aggressively and animalistically as he buries his sense of conflict by joining in with the crowd.

Crowd: No man to man ting!

Crowd & Romeo: No man to man ting!

Perry: Yo, Romeo, bro. Something is about to pop off. We're gonna move to dem Wood Green yutes, when we buck one of dem pussyholes, they're gonna get it. You need to be ready to back the beef. Ride out with the mandem, stab a man up –

Romeo: Yo bro, be easy. Why can't everyone just chill?

Perry: Go!

Romeo enters the fray, crouches down.

Yooo mandem! Bushweed yute are coming! Dip them down! Catch them! Yooo Romeo, man, get him!

Romeo pauses for a moment, conflicted. The pressure from Perry and the other boys is too much to resist.

Perry: Now, man, now!

Through a movement sequence we see the violence and an aggressive attack on another boy.

Romeo wins the spat, and he and Perry run away in celebration.

*****

Eve: Hey stranger, you alright, where you been hiding?

Romeo: *(To audience)* Eve is in the year above me at school. Every man wants her but she is on man, on it like SONIC! She wants to be my wifey and I can't think of any reason to say no.
(To Eve) Just been vybzing with the mandem.

Eve: I think it's time you started vybzing with me.

Romeo: It's like that yeah?

Eve: I'm ready you know.

A beat.

I know what I'm doing. I've done stuff before. Like hands and mouth stuff.

Romeo: *(Nervously, avoiding the situation)* Yeah, seen, seen, me too. I'mma teach you some new moves. Man's got bare experience.

Eve: Come on, let's do it then. I'm ready.

Romeo: Cool.

A beat.

Let's do this ting, I'm on it.

Another beat. Neither moves.

Eve: Well?

Romeo: Well?

Eve: What?

Romeo: What?

Eve: Don't you want to?

Romeo: I said, I'm on it.

Eve: Don't you like me?

Romeo: Course I like you.

A beat.

Eve: What's wrong with you?

Romeo: Nothing's wrong with me. Man's on this ting.

Eve: What's wrong with me?

Romeo: *(With increasing frustration)* Just relax, you're moving a bit loose.

Eve: Romeo!

Romeo: Why you pressing me?!

Eve: Come on then.

Eve and Romeo slowly and shyly make love. There's a moment of sweetness and genuine connection between them.

Romeo: *(To audience)* Afterwards I feel like I'm a big man in the streets. Yo, man's definitely not gay! I'm cured, I am straight, I am normal. No more gay thoughts.

Aaron enters and locks eyes with Romeo. The two share a tender moment of curiosity and held eye contact.

Romeo: *(Keeping eyes locked on Aaron but speaking to audience)* New year at school brings the new boy, Aaron.

Romeo breaks eye contact, to break the tension.

Eve: Omg choong ting.

Aaron: Thanks boo.

Romeo: Keep your thong on, Eve, he ain't all that.

Aaron: Is this your man, then? Are you two a ting?

Romeo: Are you tryna move to my gyal?

Aaron: Maybe. Maybe she ain't my type.

Romeo: Don't think you're hers, likkle man.

Aaron sits in between Romeo and Eve.

Eve: So what ends you from?

Aaron: W10 but man's more than a postcode.

Eve: What's west London like?

Aaron: Much the same as here, from what I can see, except but the faces ain't as pretty.

Eve giggles.

Romeo: North London is where it's at, bro.

Aaron: That's news to me. Hopefully good news.

Eve giggles again.

Romeo: Ah shut up, Eve. Yo, Aaron, you have a trial membership to the circle. Come chill in the park with us after school, bare smoke, bare gyal, bare tunes. We're the ones you wanna hang with, trust me.

Aaron: I'll be the one to make that decision. I ain't a follower, I'm a leader.

Romeo: Bad boy, it's like that, yeah.

Aaron: Ain't it like that with you?

Romeo is lost for words.

Aaron: Too many people follow the hype.

Romeo: Is it?

Aaron: I just do me.

A beat. There's something in the air between Aaron and Romeo.

Aaron: Can I get your digits, Eve?

Eve extends her hand and Aaron hands over his phone. Meanwhile Aaron has locked eyes with Romeo.

Eve: I've given you my MySpace as well. And my MSN.

Eve hands his phone back. Aaron waits on Romeo.

Romeo: *(Taken aback)* Oh yeah, safe.

Romeo takes Aaron's phone and enters his number. Aaron takes it back and presses 'call' so Romeo's phone rings. Romeo's personalised ringtone, 'Believe' - Cher', plays. Romeo is embarrassed.

Romeo: *(To audience)* My brother is always on at me to hang with the mandem, and I'm doing it, I'm a big man in these streets.

Jermaine: Big man is it?

Romeo: Who the fuck is this?

Mum: You know we don't cuss in this house!
This is Jermaine, your new… uncle.

Romeo: 'Uncle'? I don't like him.

Mum: You don't know him. Go on, stop being silly, say hello.

Romeo: No.

Mum: You think you're a big man? The shit you and Perry bringing to my yard. I can't make a cup of tea in peace, stress in my left breast. Don't make me fetch my rass belt.

Jermaine: It's cool, Marina. Let me and the likkle man have a chat.

Marina leaves.

Jermaine: I know you're becoming a big man now. And you know what big men do, they look out fi dem family, keep dem safe.

Romeo: I'm not the one that brings trouble to the yard, that's Perry. I'm just doing what I need to do.

Jermaine: *(Smooth and friendly. Determined to get Romeo on side)* Yeah, mi see that. You and me both know you're the good one. I'll speak to your mudda and I'll have a chat with your brudda. He's the one who needs fi fix up. Your mudda's been through a lot and she deserves to be happy. So help mi out and we can get your brudda on board.

Romeo warms slightly to Jermaine.

Jermaine: Mi know you don't need another father, I'm here, as a bredrin.

Jermaine hands Romeo a Guinness and they crack it open together and cheers.

Mum: What you two a chat 'bout?

Jermaine: Just big man tings. Come na, gyal.

'Night Nurse' – Gregory Isaacs plays. Jermaine and Mum dance together flirtatiously and very close. Romeo watches in horror.

Romeo: Errr, 'llow it, how you lot moving like that? Perry, Perry, come make them stop.
(To audience) It's like watching dinosaurs mating. My grandma is not impressed.

Grandma: *(Outraged)* This one only wants his bludclart stay inna England! He's thinking of his new British passport, not about you. Take the wool off ya eyes! You're too fool fool. Them nasty raas yardies, every one of dem is raas-clart pussy-clart dutty vampires.

Mum: You don't even know him, Mummy! He's a good man. Give him a chance.

Grandma: I know you, though, I know what you need. I carried you for nine months. I pushed you out of MY pussy.

Mum: Are you even listening? I love him.

Grandma: 'Love him'? You've known him three months! Three months and you're going to bring that nasty, dutty man around my grandchildren? You're making yet another mistake!

Mum: And ten years ago when I came to you that night, my nose and lip buss up, you told me to stay with their father because you said he would look after us.

Grandma: *(A lie and she knows it)* Lie you ah tell! Stop telling lies pon me!

Mum: You said it, Mummy! You only liked him for what he had to offer you! Cause he bought you expensive curtains and put central heating in your yard!

Grandma: He was a good man, him did have class.

Mum: Broken jaw, half dead, that's some class! Jermaine

might not have much to offer you but he's a good man.

Grandma: You have fi know how to choose dem, work dem and hold dem. If you're serving the pum-pum right, they behave. Not dashing out your gyash to some dutty bruck pocket man.

Mum: I love him. And Jermaine loves me.

Grandma: And I'll be there in di middle of di night when dis one starts giving you some rass licks.

*****

Romeo: Mum, you okay?

Mum: *(Showing a brave face to her son)* I'm alright darlin'. Just watching my show.

Romeo: Can I do your nails?

Mum: Go on then.

A moment of calm as they return to their old habit.

Mum: *(With warmth)* This is nice. *(Teasing)* You're growing too fass. I bet you don't tell your friends you like painting Mummy's nails.

Romeo: Mum...

Mum: Okay, okay, mi darlin'. Mummy loves you so much, you know. You and Perry will always be my likkle pickney even though you're growing and getting out there, doing all sorts that I certainly don't want to know about.

Romeo: MUM!

Mum: You tink I wasn't your age once?!

Romeo: Allow it mum.

Mum: How's school? You paying attention? Working hard?

Romeo: Yeah.

Mum: I hope so. My beautiful boy, my clever boy, you going to make Mummy proud.

A moment of gentle peace.

Romeo: Grandma will chill.

Mum: She won't. I know what she's like. My mum ain't easy. That's why I show you as much love as I do. I refuse to be the kind of mother she was.

Romeo: No one's like you, Mum.

Jermaine enters.

Jermaine: Marina, mi just finish fix di brakes pon the car so we can go fi dat likkle drive, baby love.
What ah gwan here?

Jermaine inspects Mum's nails for a moment. He ruffles Romeo's hair a little too roughly.

Jermaine: He's too old to be painting his mother's nails. He needs to harden up and stop move soft.

Mum is surprised at Jermaine's comments. Jermaine's true colours are beginning to show.

Mum: Stop your noise.

Romeo: I ain't soft. Far from.

Jermaine: You need fi start flexing like a real man.

Romeo: I am a real man.

Jermaine laughs.

Jermaine: Exactly. That's why mi no waan people think you are a likkle chi chi man. I hear when the boys call you a sodomite.

Romeo: Fuck them, I ain't like that.

The atmosphere has changed. The calm and peace between Mum and Romeo has disappeared. Jermaine jokes, but the jokes are threatening. He is showing a side of himself that Romeo and Mum have not seen before.

Jermaine: *(With an edge)* That's what I tell them when they make jokes about you. *(Making a grotesque joke which amuses himself)* I know you would never be like dem batty boys who dig out each other doo doo pans.

A beat.

Go fetch mi a Guinness ina di fridge mi boy.

Romeo: I'm not your boy. You drink too much.

Jermaine: What you say?

Romeo: Nothing.

Jermaine: You know I love your mudda.

Romeo: Yeah, whatever.

Jermaine: I want to love you and Perry too

Romeo: Whatever. I've got homework.

Romeo goes to leave. Jermaine goes to stop him.

Jermaine: Your mudda says you've always loved school.

Romeo: I guess.

Jermaine: That's good. You and Perry, smart boys.

Romeo: Mum is smart, too.

Jermaine: You tink mi don't know that?

Romeo: Dunno.

Jermaine: Mi want tek care of you all, Perry, your mudda, you. Mek sure you grow up right. Else there could be trouble.

Romeo senses Jermaine is referring to Romeo's perceived feminine or camp ways.

Jermaine: *(A subtle mild threat)* We need to mek sure you're safe. The world is a rough place. Man up.

Romeo: *(To audience)* There's no place for me at home so I cut loose.

*****

Romeo finds himself outside Aaron's window.

Romeo: Aaron, Aaron, you there bro?

Aaron's face appears.

Aaron: Yoo, bro, you good?

Romeo: Come down, yeah. My new stepdad or whatever he thinks he is, he's pissing me off.

Aaron: I feel ya bro. My 'new uncle' is doing my head in. I'm coming down.

Romeo: *(To audience)* I'm always thinking of ways for it to be the two of us.

Aaron joins Romeo.

Aaron: What you saying?

Romeo: Who's this for?!

Aaron: Who's what for?!

Romeo: This look, this whole vibe.

Aaron: I take pride in my appearance innit.

Romeo: You got your eye on someone?

Aaron: Wouldn't you like to know.

Romeo kisses his teeth.

A beat. There's tension between them.

Romeo: *(To audience)* We bop through the dark estate. Occasionally our shoulders brush, by accident. We're walking in silence and it's nice, I don't want us to speak.

Aaron: This way.

Romeo: He leads me to the top of an abandoned tower block and now we're looking out across London. Up here, everything looks so still.

Aaron: This city is ours, you know that, right?

Romeo: I feel light, like, weightless, like there's all this space inside me.

Romeo: *(To audience)* I stay at Grandma's to avoid Jermaine. My grandma plays the conservative card but she sells weed under the counter. She's sitting in her favourite chair, drinking a cup of tea and smoking a spliff.

Grandma: Tell mi about school.

Romeo: It's alright.

Grandma: You going to be a doctor and mek Grandma proud?

Romeo: I'm really enjoying drama club actually. I want to be a performer, a dancer. Something creative –

Grandma: Bwoy, why you waste your time wid dat foolishness? You need a proper job! Tings like dat don't happen for people like wi. You promise mi you'll forget all this nonsense and study hard and be a lawyer, an accountant, an engineer or a nice handsome doctor. The gyal dem love doctor!

Romeo: Yes, Grandma.

Grandma: How are tings at your mudda's?

Romeo: Jermaine still stressing me out.

Grandma: Pay that bruk pocket man no mind. He won't last. I tek his kindness, but mi laugh after him. He will never be able fi walk in your fada shoes, that was a real gentleman like your granfada.

Romeo: But Grandma –

Grandma: Just hush your mout'. Everyting will work out. You've always been different to da rest. If only your granfada was still around tings would be different. God rest him soul, Mr Campbell was di love of mi life. He was a man of quality and sophistication. Tall, dark, dapper, slim and handsome like you. He was respected by everyone inna di area. Him was a sound man, a deejay, owned a club inna di West End. There was no sound like the Campbell sound, mi tell you. He use to hussle on the side and sell a likkle bit of weed by da pound. Anyting mi and our pickney needed he would provide, as it should be.

Romeo: So grandad was a drug dealer as well?

Grandma: He was an entrepreneur! Independent businessman. Him did smart too, booksmart! He was da one dat brought mi to England and pushed mi fi go study and become a midwife. When we would argue and I use to tell him about his clart he would say, 'Gyal don't mek mi affi put mi hands pon you,' then just shake me a bit and leave. I'm telling you Romeo, all di women dem wanted a piece of him. When I use to go to his sound system events all the women would flock him and I would let dem dance and gwan wid him and I'd be doing my own ting, winding up 'pon the mandem. I knew he was coming back home wid mi.

This is a familiar story to Romeo, and he joins Grandma in reciting.

Romeo/Grandma: I was the wife and I wore di ring.

Grandma: Ooo, I miss dat man. Sometimes I look up to da sky and say, 'Leroy Campbell! Why you just sitting up there watching all this shit happen to me?' But that's life and so it goes. But then mi realise he left mi you, and you're going to get a good job, marry a nice gyal, pay your grandmudda's mortgage and mek your grandfadda proud.

Romeo: *(To audience)* Later that night, Aaron is waiting for me in the park.

Aaron: What you sayin', my G.

Romeo: All good, brudda. You?

(To audience) When he looks at me it's a rush. The world closes in and it's just the two of us. I've been dreaming and dreaming about him. Can he tell?

A moment of tension. Uncertain and thrilled by each other's presence, they are unsure of how to behave.

Aaron brings out a spliff.

Aaron: Look what I got.

Romeo: Dammm.

Aaron: We about to get lit, jigga.

They settle in the grass and light the spliff.

Romeo: *(To audience)* We're chillin' in the warm summer night, the soft feeling of the grass on our backs, the sky, dark blue above us, the sound of cars passing in the distance.

Aaron: This weed's making me bare thoughtful. What you sayin' about the future?

Romeo: The future?

Aaron: As in the rest of your life? You never think about it?!

Romeo: Well, obviously you're gonna be a footballer, you're sick at football, still.

Aaron: It's the only ting I'm good at. The rest of it fucks wid my head. I reckon you could go uni, though.

Romeo: You reckon? Me, uni?!

Aaron: Yeah, you, uni. You're bare smart.

Romeo: I definitely wanna do something big. Like, acting. I used to love doing school plays in primary school.

Aaron: Swear down?

Aaron smiles at the thought of this.

Aaron: Go on then, what you got?

Romeo: 'Tis torture and not mercy. Heaven is here, Where Juliet lives, And every cat and dog And little mouse, Every unworthy thing, Live here in heaven and may look on her, But Romeo may not.

Romeo is shy. Aaron is amused and into it.

Romeo: Don't laugh.

Aaron: I ain't laughing, I'm smiling. That's lit, my G. Sometimes I get tired of people chatting shit 24/7. Tell me something real that's gonna get mans out of the hood, like real talk.

Romeo: I lie, I love the brotherhood, we look out for each other, party together, fight together, protect each other. But what's next? Goin' prison together, dying together, where's the love and freedom in that? I want more. Better things for myself, for all of us. I just don't know how.

A beat.

Aaron: You should be like this when other people are about, like chill. Instead of always putting on a front.

Romeo: You know how the roadz go.

Aaron: Can't we just be real and fuck everyone else?

Romeo: I feel like I can only talk to you like this.

Aaron: Me too.

Romeo: Like I know you'll get it.

Aaron: I love vybzing with you, you get me?

Romeo: I get you.

Aaron: People say that all the time but, we actually are getting each other. *(Joking)* You get me?

Romeo is silent. Aaron reaches out and touches his shoulder.

Romeo: Aaron?

Aaron: Yeah?

Romeo: *(To audience)* He looks at me, and in that moment, the burst of love, I know there's no going back. This is the beginning of everything.

A tender movement sequence during the following dialogue as they explore their first intimacy.

Aaron: Is this okay?

Romeo: Yeah, it's good.

Aaron: Can I touch you here?

Romeo: Yeah, yeah

Aaron: This is good, like, this feels really good.

Romeo: But we're not gay.

Aaron: Just horny.

Romeo: We like girls.

Aaron: Bare girls like you, Romeo.

Romeo: Come on my G! Girls like it when I do this. Do you like it?

Aaron: That feels good.

Romeo: You like that?

Aaron: It's soo good. Tell me what you want me to do to you.

Romeo: I want…

Aaron: Use your words.

Romeo: I want to go next level.

Aaron: What's next level?

Romeo: You. I want you.

Aaron: Tell me.

Romeo: All of you.

(To audience) He holds me down.

Romeo and Aaron share a deep intake of breath.

Romeo: It's a moment of heaven.

Movement sequence ends.

Romeo: We make our way home, the darkness hides us.

Aaron: You good, yeah?

Romeo: Yeah, I'm good. You good?

Aaron: Yeah, yeah. I'm good.

Romeo: We're good.

Romeo reaches down in the darkness takes Aaron's hand and intertwine a couple of fingers.

Romeo: *(To audience)* Lucky for us one of the streetlamps is out so we're still protected by the shadows.

As we approach the Lightfoot Estate I can make out a crowd surrounding my door. Blue lights are flashing, pulsing.

Panic rising, Aaron lets go of Romeo's hand. Steps away.

Romeo: You coming?

Aaron: Nah. Call me, yeah?

Romeo: *(To audience)* Terror rises in me and I start to run. My front door is in full sight now and I can see... that there's a policewoman... standing there... next to my mum.

Light change. Mood shift. The company joins Romeo on-stage to show a fairground ride.

Romeo: *(To audience)* Every year Perry and I go to the funfair that comes to Priory Park. There's this one ride called a Gravitron, it's our favourite. You stand in a drum and it starts to spin, until your whole body is pressed to the wall. Then the ground drops away from below your feet. The world is spinning but you're stuck there, hardly able to move. That is Mum and me, right now, in the back of a police car… No gravity. Stuck.

We pull up to the hospital car park and see one of my brother's friends crying, wailing, losing his shit. By the time we enter the ICU we're both shaking.

And there's Perry, covered in a thousand tubes. His face all swollen. His head is fucking huge.

I can feel my heart beating in my skull, my veins boiling, rupturing. My chest is tight, it hurts to breathe. I see crimson, I want blood. I want to bust out of there and fuck someone up, do what they've done to him.

Romeo goes to leave. Grandma stops him.

Grandma: Romeo Randall Campbell! Where you tink you goin'? Come here, come here now and kneel with mi, mi boy. Look at your brudda laying there lifeless, if you don't buckle up you will be next! Do what mi tell you! Your mum's been through enough, you're putting mi daughter in an early grave, you have social services a call, threatening, saying we don't know how to raise our children, putting a bad name on the family.

Grandma and Romeo kneel and pray together.

Grandma: Dear Lord, cover your lamb in your flesh, blood and holy spirit. Shine your light pon dis 'ere hospital room. No evil shall prosper under the gaze of your almighty compassion and protection. Strike down the devil and drive him out. Drive him out!

Romeo: Amen.

Grandma: Out, devil!

Grandma begins flicking her religious oils around the room and leaping.

Grandma: Out Lucifer! Out demon. Come out of dis room, come out of the body and mind of mi baby, out of the lives of dis family, out of the grounds of dis hospital.

Jesus, Lord, forgive these children for their sins and transgressions. They do not know the chains and shackles that were set before their time, but as their spiritual nurturer, I will teach them to humble themselves before di Almighty. Together we will overcome and pray the evil spirit from our door.

Not today, Satan, not today Grim Reaper, out! Mi say out!

Romeo: *(To audience)* Grandma still swears it was her prayers that saved him. All I know is, by the grace of God – whatever that means to you; I know what it means to me – my brother recovered in a week.

All I can think about is getting back to Aaron.

Aaron: Yo, man, where you been?

Romeo: Where you been?

Aaron: I been busy, innit.

Romeo: Busy ghosting me?

Aaron: Why you chattin' shit, bro?

Romeo: Really 'bro'?

Aaron: 'Llow it, man.

Romeo: You what?

Aaron: Just leave me alone, G.

Romeo: What the fuck?

Aaron: I'm not on dem tings anymore. I can't have anyone

knowing about what *(lowers voice)* happened with us. Swear you won't tell no one, yeah.

Romeo: Who am I gonna tell? I done it too.

Aaron: Swear to me.

A beat. Romeo is heartbroken but determined to hide it.

Romeo: Aaron…

Aaron: *(Becoming aggressive)* Fucking swear!

Romeo: *(Shaken)* I swear.

A beat.

Aaron: Cool, well catch you around.

Romeo: I should've been with Perry that night. He needed me. I could've protected him. I wasn't there when he needed me.

A beat.

Aaron: Perry does what Perry wants.

Romeo: Aaron, I –

Aaron: I need to get back

Romeo: Why are you doing this?

Aaron: *(Laughing it off)* I ain't doing nothing.

Romeo is crushed.

*****

Romeo: *(To audience)* Perry won't go to school or leave the house. He sits and stares into space with the curtains drawn.

Romeo takes a deep breath.

Romeo: You wanna walk to the shops?

Perry: Nah.

Romeo: Might be good for you to get some air or –

Perry: I can't.

Romeo: It's literally just round the corner –

Perry: I said no.

Romeo: Come on man –

Perry: Allow it.

Romeo: Fine. We'll just sit here...

A beat.

Romeo: Put on a beat and drop some bars, man, show me what you've been working on.

Perry: Stop getting on to me, bro.

Romeo: Ahh shut up man, I'm here tryna help.

Perry: I don't give a shit. I didn't arx for help.

Romeo: You're moving like a bitch. It's not my fault you got stabbed, not such a big man after all.

Perry: Shut the fuck up you lil poof, you would never of survived it.

Romeo: That's what you think, you mad prick.

Perry: Suck your mum –

Romeo: Suck your mum... You stupid, selfish dickhead. You've caused us all so much stress. You've ruined my life, do you know that? And still you're acting like this. You could've died. Imagine what that would have done to Mum.

Perry: You think I don't think about that?!
(Beat) What are people saying about me?

Romeo: Nothing, man.

Perry: What have you told them?

Romeo: I ain't told nobody shit.

Perry: You told them I'm scared to go out?

Romeo: Fuck's sake, no.

Perry: I ain't scared, yunno. It's just – it's all bullshit out there. You know.

Romeo: Oh, my gosh, Perry, man, stop bunning so much weed, seriously, it's not helping, it's fucking with your head.

Perry ignores Romeo and presses on.

Perry: That's why people are arxing questions, getting in my business, cause they're still out to get me.

Romeo: What are talking about, fam?

Perry: No one rates me anymore. They all think I'm moist. The second I drop my guard they'll come for me.

35

I heard a car pass last night, blasting a track, they were sending me a message. Next time you won't survive, next time we'll fucking end you.

Romeo: Okay, okay, relax man. It's okay, I got you, I'm here.

Romeo embraces Perry and Perry is momentarily soothed. Perry clings on and sobs.

Romeo: I got you. I promise, I got you, bro.

Romeo holds Perry tight. For a moment we see them as they were as children.

Perry: I got you too, bro.

A beat.

Perry: So what about your ting?

Romeo: What you chatting about?

Perry: When you gonna tell mum you like it up the batty innit?

Romeo: Shut ya mout'!

Perry: I'll shut my mout' if you open up yours and act like a man. You've always been braver than me.

Romeo: Alright, Nelson Mandela.

Perry: Stop movin' like a pussy and chat to mum.

*****

Romeo: Mum. I'm gay.

A beat.

Mum: I know.

Romeo: How did you know?

Mum: I've always known.

Romeo: Since when?

Mum: From when you was a little pickney. I told Auntie Viv.

Romeo: Why didn't you say nothing?

Mum: I was waiting for you to tell me.

Romeo: You should've said something,

Mum: Like what?

Romeo: Like 'it's okay if you're gay'. Rahh I thought I was doing a good job hiding it but all these years you've known.
You know what? I want an apology.

Mum: For what?

Romeo: For letting Jermaine and everyone make all them sly jabs chatting all that 'chi chi man' shit.

Mum: Jermaine's gone, so problem solved.

Mum is attempting to avoid this conversation. She's embarrassed. Years of shame and fear are released as Romeo talks openly to his mother for the first time.

Romeo: That's not the point and you know it. You stood there and let him say all that and now you're telling me that you knew.

Mum: *(Defensive)* Romeo get over it. You're gay, I love you, move on.

Romeo: Do you know how hard it is hearing them things? The things that everyone says. Why don't you stand up for me?

Mum is silent.

Romeo: Mum why you ignoring me?
Mum.
Fuck's sake.

Mum: Romeo, watch your mouth.

A long beat.

Mum: *(This is hard for her to say)* I'm worried about how hard life will be for you. Being like that, being different. I'm not stupid.

Romeo: Well, you should make it better, that's your job. Instead you let Jermaine chat shit to me like that? Making me hate myself.

Mum: You're not the only one who needs looking after.

Romeo: You let everyone chat shit. You deserted me when I needed you, do you know how hard this has been for me, thinking I'm broken, thinking I'm something to be ashamed of, thinking that people will hate me, beat me, want me dead like in the songs that I've heard played in my own house my whole life, Mum, I'm scared.

Mum: I'm sorry! I'm sorry Romeo. I'm so sorry.

They both hug.

Romeo: It's okay, Mum. Don't cry, don't cry...

Mum: I'm scared too. I love you, I would die for you, I would do anything, but I didn't know what to say.

Romeo: *(To audience)* Truth is I needed to see her cry. I've walked through the fire and survived. What I didn't realise was this was just a spark and the real fire was to come.

The soundscape of distant muffled club beats builds to a

crescendo until the stage explodes into darkness.

ACT TWO

Club music plays.

Romeo: *(To audience)* Welcome to My 18th birthday. I'm dressed up, all white, keeping it subtle. White fur jacket, white crop top, white batty riders. And Auntie Viv's daughter Chardonnay, my favourite cousin, is my partner in crime.

Char: HAPPY BIRTHDAY BITCH!

Romeo: Am I really doing this, Char?

Char: Not this again! It's happening, babes. You're finally legal, you've got backoff like a perky ripe peach and we're going out out!

Romeo and Char wait nervously in the queue.

Romeo: What if we see someone I know and they ask me, 'What you doin' here?'

Char: You reply back, 'Same thing as you, bitch'! Just wait, gyal, you'd be surprised which niggas and bitches from endz are batting for your team.

Romeo psyches himself up.

Romeo: Thank you, Char.

Char: I got you. You know I'll cut a bitch for you. We run these motherfucking streets.

Char/Romeo: Period!

'My Neck, My Back' – Khia plays loud.

Romeo: *(To audience)* We head inside. The music and the shadows suck me in. We've walked into the den and the dogs are licking their lips with searching hungry eyes. Everyone looks so... gay. I hear black voices on the sound system but all I can see around me are white faces, ugh – HEAVEN.

Char: Don't piss your nappy. This was just the warm up. Come we go. TAXI!

Romeo: *(To audience)* Bootylicious – but we call it Booty!

Movement sequence celebrating the black gay scene. Music: 'Throat' – Gage.

Romeo: Finally, my people!

Glittering black bodies shimmering under lights.
Moving together like an unstoppable wave breaking over the rocks on the shore.
I'm lost in it.
I'm found in it.

The bodies merge into one sweating, writhing, sensual black cloud.
I dance for all the men that went before me
The ones that weren't permitted.
We breathe together.
Sweat trickling as I dance with the ghosts of the lost men who never got to dance like this.
Who lived in homes that weren't their homes at all.
Who lived as fictional versions of themselves
Forced to pretend.
Because the world told them they had to hide.
Through us they finally get to live
Free

Every night.
Can you see it? Are you in my world now?

Music: 'Flap Your Wings' – Nelly.

Floating through the night
Nothing matters but this moment.
Checking me out, are you?
You love how I look, how I dance.
You want me. I can see it in your eyes.
See me dance, tease and flirt with men who queue up to take my pretty pussy home.
Sorry, not sorry – you can't have me, you can't own me.
I don't need to be in your clique – or yours. I'm just doing Romeo's ting.
Buy me a drink, or two, but you won't get me.
You'll never get me.
Put the lines out.
You know we'll have a good time, but you can't buy this bussy.
I ain't ready to follow through yet.
You can have a little taste of my sugar, sure, but you know I'm going to be moving on to the next and the next.
Bye, Next, Bye, Next, Bye –

From the crowd, Sami, Romeo's next love, appears.

Music: a mash-up of 'Flap Your Wings' – Nelly, and 'Turn and Wine' – Vybz Kartel.

Sami: Hi.

Romeo: *(To audience)* It's like he's parting the seas like Jesus. Dressed in fur head to toe, bare chest, gold and pearls.

Sami: So you got a name?

Romeo: Might do... It's Romeo.

Sami: Suits you.

Romeo: I've heard that before.

Sami: But never from a guy like me.

Romeo: Ain't you gonna ask if it's real? People always ask.

Sami: You look like a Romeo to me.

Romeo: So what's your name?

Sami: Guess. Ponder it, I'll be back.

Sami begins to walk off. Romeo calls him back.

Romeo: Oy! Baby, *you* approached *me*.

Sami: And maybe I will again, baby.

Sami begins to walk off again.

Romeo: Is that how you're playing it?

Sami: I don't play games, baby, I prefer extreme sports.

Romeo: Bad boy, yeah.

Sami shrugs.

You gonna tell me or not?

Sami: It's Sami with an 'i'.

Sami laughs to himself.

Romeo: What?

Sami: Oh, baby, you're gorgeous when you're confused.

Romeo laughs.

Saimi: Even more so when you laugh.

Romeo: *(To audience)* We fall hard and we fall fast.

Sami: Give me a kiss, baby, I'm thirsty.

Romeo: We're in Stratford bus station, are you crazy?
(To audience) But Sami don't care. He leans in and kisses
me and in that moment I think, I'm not scared anymore.

*Movement sequence with Romeo and Sami's dialogue below
as they explore intimacy and make love for the first time.*

Romeo: I love touching you there.

Sami: Yeah, yeah. Like it when I do this?

Romeo: That feels really good.

Sami: And this.

Romeo: That's good.

Romeo's nervousness begins to build.

Sami: I love you.

Romeo: You do?

Sami: Yeah, I do.

Romeo: Really?

Sami: Yeah.

Romeo: I love you, too.

Sami: I love you.

Romeo: I want you.

Sami: Can I go in?

Romeo: I want all of you.

Movement sequence ends.

Romeo: *(To audience)* I'm home in his arms.

*****

Mum: Good morning, your highness.

Viv: Fuck me, you look mash up, late night was it?

Romeo: Please lower your tones.

Mum: I tell you, Viv, this boy of mine he's in love.

Viv: You met any other nice men for me? If you have any left over, send them my way.

Romeo: Yes, auntie.

Viv: I tell you the gays love me, always have.

Mum: Hush, Viv. Don't get distracted with raving and man.

Viv: She's right.

Romeo: Yes, yes.

Mum: I'm serious. we need to look at some options for you.

Viv: Yes, Marina, you're right. She's right, Romeo.

Romeo: Can you two give me a break!

Mum: Live under my roof, do as I say. I've been there, done it, bought the batty riders.

Romeo: You lot are so annoying. I'm going back to bed.

Mum: Don't get too caught up in love, you've got bigger fish to fry. You're a smart boy, you should be studying.

Viv: And remember what I said, you have any men spare, send them my way. I've got a hole to fill.

Romeo: YOU LOT NEED TO 'LLOW IT.

Romeo goes to walk off.

Viv: And don't forget to fill your own hole!

Romeo: *(Mortified)* Auntie Viv!

Viv: Or fill someone else's – whatever your ting is!

Romeo escapes Mum and Viv in the kitchen and joins Perry.

Romeo: Them lot need to 'llow it.

Perry: Yo, the mandem wants me to come do a black box session on Urban TV.

Romeo: Why you associating with them? Where were they when you was lying on a hospital bed fighting for your life?

Perry: They've been riding out revenging me.

Romeo: Really?!

Perry: Shut up, man! Listen to this verse I wrote.

Romeo rolls his eyes as Perry plays the song from his phone.

Perry: *(Rapping)* I'm a real badman in the rave
You're a likkle joke, man play games
Can't listen to the tune and say same
I'm all about the hustle, you're all about the fame
Man don't dance, I just stand and screw
So remember who you're talking to
Don't watch face when I'm walking through
Last thing you hear is click click boom
Way too cold, I'm icy
I'm coming for you and your wifey
And if the jury wanna know if I'm guilty
I'mma say I just might be

Romeo vibes to the track.

Romeo: Perry that is sick! But does it have to be so negative?

Perry: I'm just spitting my reality.

Romeo: Don't get drawn back into those boys. They're not good for you.

Perry: Leave it, I know what I'm doing.

Romeo: You been smoking?

Perry: No.

Romeo: Perry...

Perry: Go on, run back to your boyfriend.

Romeo: *(To audience)* And I do. Days with Sami melt into nights...

*****

Sami and Romeo in bed. That post-coital glow.

Romeo: When did you first know?

Sami: Since always.

Romeo: It took me a while, like I didn't know what this was.

Sami: You buried it.

Romeo: Nah, it just didn't cross my mind.

Sami: *(Teasing)* Yeah, cause you buried it.

Romeo: Who was your first?

Sami: My cousin's friend. My dad caught us. He hasn't spoken to me since.

Romeo: I don't know how my dad would react, but my mum's cool.

Sami: I wish I had what you have. I want to have a kid and be the dad I never had.

Romeo: You do?!

Sami: Not any time soon, but yeah. Show them all the love. Dad tried to beat the queer out of me. Mum tried to pray it away. Took a while to realise I wasn't completely broken.

Romeo: You're perfect.

Sami: Who was your first?

Romeo: This boy joined our school in year 10 and he was…

Sami: …hot?

Romeo: DL, straight, whatever, I thought we was a ting and then he ice-cold ghosted me.

Sami: I never go near straight boys. Forget about curious,

they're all obsessed. In the end it's not worth it. Next!

Romeo: I wanted to fuck him up.

Sami: *(Hugging him)* Come here…

Romeo: The shame. How dare he?!

Sami: Fuck shame!

Romeo: You've obviously never had it.

Sami: You have to pity these DL boys. That anger is only going to fuck you up, not them.

Romeo: *(To audience)* It was me and Sami against the world. But you lot remember what it's like to be nineteen and in love. Things change between us, too quick. Where did that feeling go, that rush that brought us together? I want it to come back but it won't. My eyes begin to wander. I want everyone and everythin'. I start to meet up with others. Is Sami doing the same?

Sami places his arm around Romeo, kissing his neck.

Sami: Why you flinching?

Romeo: I'm not.

Sami: I thought you liked me touching you.

Romeo: I do.

Sami: Come here then.

Sami initiates intimacy. Romeo shrugs him off.

Sami: What?!

Romeo: Give me a minute, man.

A beat. Sami tries again to begin intimacy. Again, Romeo shrugs him off.

Sami: What is it?

Romeo: Let me breathe, innit.

Sami: Where was you last night?

Romeo: Out.

Sami: With who?

Romeo: Why you being like this?

Sami: You're a fuck boy.

Romeo: But you love it.

Sami: Tell me where you were.

Romeo: Stop getting on to me. You approached me, remember?

Sami: You think I don't know what you've been doing, running around behind my back, it ain't cute.

Romeo: I'd rather be running around than lying around all day, that ain't sexy. You're a bum.

Sami goes to leave.

Sami: And this bum's out.

Romeo: Don't you dare walk away from me.

Sami: Look at you and then look at me.

Romeo: You serious?

Sami: Everyone wants me, do you know how lucky you are?

Romeo: As if. Ask anyone, you're old news.

Sami: You petty little boy. You're so messed up, you know that. No wonder your dad left you.

This riles Romeo. It's a sore point and Sami knows it.

Sami: I didn't mean that.

Romeo: At least my family accepts me. Why you acting like such a bitch?

Sami: What's wrong with being a bitch?

Romeo: But you're a scared little bitch.

Sami goes to walk away.

Romeo: That's right, walk away little bitch.

Sami: What you going to do, big man?

Romeo pushes Sami in the head. Sami pushes Romeo, who goes down, then jumps up.

Sami: Shit!

Romeo: I'm good, it's alright.

They relent. Heartbroken, but both refusing to admit it.

Sami: Just because we're boys, doesn't make it alright. Did I hurt you?

Romeo: FUCK OFF!

Mum storms in.

Sami exits.

Mum: Why you bringing drama into my yard?
(Notices Romeo's tears)
Oh my baby, don't cry, come here.

Romeo: Leave me, I'm a big man. I can handle my own shit.

Mum: Course you can handle it. You don't want him anyway. Come here, come to Mummy.

Romeo shrugs his mum away.

Romeo: You don't get it.

Mum: Get what? What more do you want from me?

Romeo: You don't understand.

Mum: Of course I get it, baby, come here.

Romeo: You're not listening to me.

Mum: What?

Romeo: Everyone's always hassling me, putting pressure on me. Just leave me the fuck alone.

Mum: Romeo Campbell, you watch your mouth.

Romeo: This is what I mean!

Mum: I'm just trying to help!

Romeo: I don't want you to! I can't live here anymore. It's time I lived my own life in peace.

Mum: Gwan then. You won't find anyone who'll put up wid your nonsense like me.

Romeo: Fine. I'm out.

Mum: *(Thrusting a bag at him)* Let me help you pack.

*****

Perry enters high as a kite and aggressive.

Perry: Yo yo yo bro, I finally got the drop on the yute that bored man. Come let's go!

Romeo: I thought we spoke 'bout dis.

Perry: And I made it clear I'mma get mine.

Romeo: Come out my face, you're buzzing. I ain't got time for this.

Perry: I need you, bro.

Romeo: Just stay home and chill.

Perry: I can't. I told you, people are watching me.

Romeo: No one is watching you. The weed is making you paro.

Perry: Have they got to you as well?

A beat.

Romeo: What are you talking about?

Perry's paranoia and dissociation from reality is growing.

Perry: I told you he's coming for man. I ain't gonna be caught lackin' again!

Perry reveals to Romeo that he is carrying a gun. Romeo is instantly terrified and freezes up.

Romeo: Bro have you lost your mind!? Why've you got dat in Mum's house?

Perry: I'm just holding it for someone.

Romeo: Perry.

Perry: You deaf? You're such a pussy'ole.

Romeo: Put the fucking gun away!

Perry: For what? You've all given up on me. I'm alone. You've left me, Mum's left me.

In this moment of terror we see Romeo and Perry as they were as children.

Romeo: (*Pleading like a child to his father*) Perry, Perry, please, please, 'llow it man!

Perry: Fuck it, I'mma back myself.

Romeo: Perry, Perry I am begging you, what the fuck, man?

Perry: Keep your voice down. You're such a drama queen, will you just chill?

Romeo: And you're such a fuck up. You're not a bad boy. You were never built for these streets, that's why man-dem got you holding guns in your mum's yard but not in deirs. And let's be real 'bro', you ain't gonna do shit wid dat anyway, so put it away, go back to your weed and your PlayStation!

Perry: So you ain't got man's back?

Romeo: I said what I said!

Perry: Fuck you!

Perry exits.

Romeo takes deep breaths to steady himself. He takes out his phone and tries to call Perry, panic rising.

Romeo: Come on, come on, answer.

The phone goes straight to voicemail:

Perry: *(VO)* I'm a real badman in the rave
    You're a likkle joke, man play games…

    Leave a message.

Romeo fights back tears.

*****

Romeo phones Chardonnay.

Char: S'up bitch?

Romeo: Char, knickers on tits out, we're going club?

Char: It's a Tuesday night, babes. I got work tomorrow.

Romeo: Stop being a boring bitch, come out.

Char: Your mum's worried, Romeo. She said you had a bust up?

Romeo: I don't care, I've had enough. Just come the fuck out.

Char: I gotta get some rest. It's not an every day party. I'll call you tomorrow.

Romeo: Wait, wait, Char babes, can you call Perry and check he's okay?

Char: Honestly, you two. I'm busy, I've got shit to be getting on with!

Romeo: *Please*, Chardonnay.

Char: I'm setting my boundaries, babes. Call him yourself. Love you, bye!

Romeo: Bye.

Romeo hangs up.

Bitch.

*****

The company join Romeo onstage to show the following sequence through movement. They become the fellow ravers, the fellow sauna guests, the fellow chemsex party attendees. All searching for something, pushing their night to the extreme.

Romeo: That night I dance and dance.

Someone buys me a drink, someone passes me a pill. Give it all to me!

Rave, search, rave, search, rave, search.

Fuck my family, I don't need them, I can make my own family. No one's holding me back.

The lights of the club come on.

Romeo: *(To audience)* It's only 3:30 – where's the party at?

A member of the company extends a hand to Romeo.

Host: Come to Chariots.

The company surrounds Romeo as steam and smoke fill the stage.

Romeo: *(To audience)* I follow the crowd to the sauna.

Steam, heat, sweat. Eyes on me, everyone wanting me,

me, me. Bodies around me, skin skin skin.

The steam is thick and heavy, clouding the way through the never-ending maze of corridors. A different invitation behind every door.

I love how much they want me, but I can't see the way out of this place. I push open the door to a dark room full of touches and sounds.

The company performs a movement sequence.

Romeo: Touch me here, touch me there, come closer, you can do anything you want to me, that's it, don't be shy. Steam, heat, sweat. Steam, heat, sweat.
Touch me, touch me, touch me anywhere…

Come on, it's only 8 a.m.! What's next?

Romeo's Grindr sounds.

Host: Donkey Dong, dom top, here – horny and high. Great views, great guys, great gear. Party 'n' play. I'll send an Uber.

Romeo: *(To audience)* You will always remember your first chem sex party. The Uber drops you off outside an apartment building. The lift up is smooth, the doors glide open and you step into another world.

You were expecting only one guy, but it's a flat full of them.

Romeo: I thought it was gonna just be us?

Host: Just relax, enjoy.

Romeo: *(To audience)* The host passes me something and I take it. A puff of Tina becomes a pill. A line of white becomes a shot of G.

(To Host) Did you just take a picture?

(To audience) The drinks just keep flowing. There's porn on the TV and all my sexual fantasies are playing out in front of me.

Grab, stroke, spank. I can take more.

Lick, suck, swallow.

Scratch, bite, slap.

Panic rises in Romeo and he pulls away from the Host.

Romeo: *(To audience)* Just give me a minute.
(To Host) Are you filming me?

Host: Just for my wank bank. Being a little tease, are we?

Romeo: *(Trying to laugh it off)* Nah, nah, I'm just tired. Is that me on the screen?

Host aggressively grabs Romeo.

Host: You like it when I touch you there, don't you?

Romeo: No, not there.

Host: There?

Romeo: Yo stop, wait, chill out, man.

Host: Bit late to play hard to get. Come 'ere.

Romeo: I said get the FUCK OFF ME. Please, please... Get off me.

Romeo deep-breathes: revisiting the assault has affected him powerfully. He pulls himself together. The floor is slowly disappearing from underneath his feet.

Romeo: *(To audience)* Outside the window it's daytime. The sky is blinding. I find my belongings scattered around the flat. In the living room a group of guys are still on it, fucked off their faces. I try to say goodbye but I'm dead to them. I'm clothed. They want my wildness, not my truth. I charge up my phone in the filthy kitchen. As it comes to life I see hundreds of missed calls.

(To caller) Stop calling my bludclart phone!

Mum: Romeo?

Romeo: Mum. I'm busy.

Mum: It's Perry.

Romeo: It's always about Perry!

Mum: He's gone, Ro,

Romeo: What? This ain't the time for silly games.

Mum: He's been arrested.

A long terrible silence.

Mum: I've been trying to call you. *(Pause.)* What the hell is going on with you? You tink raving, drugs and banging man left right and centre is the answer? FIX UP!

Romeo: Maybe I wouldn't be like this if I'd been raised properly.

A beat.

Mum: How dare you.

Romeo: I don't need to listen to this.

Mum: Don't you dare hang up on me –

Romeo hangs up on his mum.

Lift: (VO) Going down.

Romeo stares out. He is silent for a long time.

Romeo: *(To audience)* In the lift, I look at my reflection in
the stainless steel. Blood trickling down my nose.
Pupils as big as saucers.
Dry skin,
Dark circles,
My mouth ulcerated, gums sliced open.
But I'm fine, I'm bless, I just need some rest.
Why they always getting onto me? I'm just living my life.

Romeo retches. The lift doors open.

ACT THREE

Mum's house. Grandma answers the door to Romeo.

Grandma: Lord God! It's the Grim Reaper. You got a lot of
nerve turning up like dis.

Romeo: Where's mum?

Grandma: Your mudda doesn't want fi see you.

Romeo walks in past Grandma.

Grandma: Romeo Randall Campbell don't turn your back on
your Grandmudda.

*Romeo stops opposite his mum, who seems surprised to see
him.*

 A beat.

Mum: Where you been?

Romeo: Don't be asking big man questions.

A beat.

Grandma: You see how him come inna your house looking
mash up, so?

Romeo: I'm fine.

Mum: Are you?

Romeo: *(Snapping back)* I'm the best I've ever been.

Grandma: You look like duppy!

Romeo rolls his eyes.

Romeo: Where's Perry, then?

Grandma: Go see him an' find out fi yuh dyamn self.

Mum: Where've you been, Ro?

Romeo: *(Defensive)* 'Llow it, mum, can you just shut up for once?

Grandma: Who ya tell shut up? You want mi come over deh and box you inna you mouth?

Mum: Mum, calm down.

Grandma: No, dis is why dem always ah give you stress inna your lef' breast. When you was younger you could never fix your mout' to backchat mi like dat. Mi woulda kill you wid some rass licks.

Mum: *(warning tone)* Mum, your blood pressure!

Grandma: *(Kissing her teeth)* Blood pressure mi rass.

Grandma storms off. There is a moment of silence.

Mum: You think I'm some fool.

Romeo: *(Sassy AF)* No, I think you're really smart actually.

Mum: *(On the edge of tears)* What do you want me to say? I'm a bad mum? You're young now but this, all this, what you're doing now, the way you're acting, it don't last five seconds, trust me.

Romeo: Trust you? You don't even know me! You never did!

Mum: One day you're going to wake the hell up and realise you've wasted your life and for what?!

Romeo: You don't get to tell me how to live my life when you done nothing with yours! You're no one!

Mum is taken aback and seems broken by his insults. Romeo is silent. He's shocked himself with his cruelty towards the mother he loves so much.

Mum: You can throw all your anger at me but I'm not the enemy.

Romeo remains silent.

You are a strong, vulnerable black man...

Romeo: For fucksake change the record!

Mum pushes on, ignoring Romeo's interjection.

Mum: ...and you can do anything you set your mind to.

Romeo: Maybe you should tell Perry that. He's the one that needs it.

Mum: You can fool yourself. But you can't fool life.

Mum leaves. Grandma returns. Romeo is silent and can't look her in the eye.

Grandma: Who can't hear must feel!

Grandma follows Mum out.

Romeo: *(To audience)* Whatever. Live alone, die alone, next.

*****

Prison visiting area. Romeo enters with the same roadman bravado and physicality he used to perform.

Romeo: What you sayin' bro. You holdin' it up? Let me know if anyone's messing wid you.

There is a prolonged silence between them. Romeo shrugs.

Romeo: Okay.

Romeo takes a seat across from his brother. He returns to his 'true' persona.

Romeo: Oh my god, look around, this is trade heaven. Lock me up and throw away the keys.

Perry is silent.

Hello, anyone in there?
Anyone made you their bitch yet?

A beat.

Oh my god, jokes. Gosh, just trying to make light of another situation you've landed yourself in, again.

Perry: 'Jokes'?

Romeo: You alright?

Perry: Just imagining you in here. You wouldn't last a day. You were always better than me bro. But maybe that's changed. Grandma says you're moving like a crackhead.

Romeo: That's rich coming from you.

Perry: You're so dumb, man.

Romeo: Excuse me?!

Perry: You're so lucky and you don't even know it. You got something special.

Romeo: Special? Wasn't you the one that was always telling me I needed to change?

Perry: I was stupid. I was just trying to protect you and keep you safe.

Romeo: Most of the time *I* was keeping *you* safe!

Perry: And now you're as big a mess as I am.

Romeo: But I can walk out and you're stuck in here.

Perry: And you're stuck out there. Acting like you're thriving when you're fucked.
It's over for me.

Romeo: *(Softening)* Okay drama queen, you'll be out soon enough.

Perry: To do what? Go back to the mandem?

Romeo: Fuck the mandem! They don't give a shit about you!

Perry: It ain't about the mandem. They got strengths, passions and dreams too, but just like us they're wasting it.

Romeo: Excuse me, I ain't wasting shit, and I ain't nothing like the mandem. Different leagues baby!

Perry: What about the gay mandem? Ain't that the same shit? Trying to look hard, trying to flex? Fucking every-thing that moves to make you feel like a real man? Imag-ine what you could do if you learned how to channel your talent, your energy, your power, fam. That's gold dust bro. And you're wasting it. Yeah, I'm finished. And you're next.

Romeo: Stop tryna put your bad juju energy on me. I'm far from next.

Perry: Is that all you heard? Are you listening to me?

Romeo: When the fuck did anyone ever listen to *me*?

Perry: I'm listening. What you got to say?

Silence.

The bell rings, signalling it's time for Romeo to go.

Perry: Shout me when you've grown, yeah?

Romeo: *(To audience)* Family. Who needs them. Friends, lovers, people... who needs any of them. Born alone, die alone. Next!

Romeo is alone and vulnerable with the audience. He speaks directly to us.

What you lot looking at? What? I'm good. I'm fine. You hear me. I'm fine. I'm fine. What? Would you rather me cry myself to sleep? Bun that.

I'm fine.

I am fine.

Suddenly out of nowhere, southbound at Finsbury Park, facing each other as two grown men, me and Aaron. And I'm back where it all began.

They observe each other for a long moment.

Aaron: What you saying bro?

Romeo: Not much, you?

Aaron: I'm with QPR these days.

Romeo: Football just like you said. Nice one bro.

Aaron: Thanks, man.

A beat.

You know I've got a kid now.

Romeo: Congratulations.

Aaron: A little girl. She's a handful.

A beat.

Romeo: You been banging gym, yeah?

Aaron: Yeah man, they work us hard. How about you, you still doing drama and that?

Romeo: *(Lying to make himself look better)* Yeah, I am. Got a banging agent.

Aaron: Nice one.

Romeo decides to continue his lie.

Romeo: There's bare drama schools that want me, they've been proper fighting over me. I had an audition last week, lots of auditions, all these directors and, like, film people. My phone won't stop ringing.

Aaron: I ain't surprised.

A beat. The air is loaded with the history of what happened between them.

Aaron: You always had that... spark. Different from the rest. It's hard innit, to ignore these voices in your head telling you there's something wrong with you. *(The following is hard for Aaron to say)* I heard you came out.

A beat.

Aaron: Proud of you, still.

Romeo has a moment of realisation about his self-respect and everything he's achieved.

Romeo: Yeah, me too.

Aaron: You're doing it all. You've got it all going on.

Romeo: Yeah, I do.

Aaron: Takes courage.

A beat.

Aaron: I'm sorry for how I left things with you back then. I was scared. I went through a lot last year with my mental health and it gave me time to like, reflect and that. I'm better now, it's all good.

Romeo doesn't know what to say.

Romeo: Anyway, I'm running late. Let's link up sometime.

Aaron: Yeah, safe bro, see you around.

Romeo: *(To audience)* He still wanted me, innit?

All these DL boys who never come out, wifey at home and on Grindr at night, living a lie. Sad. Lonely. Lost. ....Pathetic.

A beat.

Romeo is alone and vulnerable with the audience. He speaks directly to us once more. There's a feeling that the audience is getting closer to Romeo, we're seeing him as he is with nowhere to hide.

Romeo: *(To audience)* Who are you lot judging? I'm living my truth unlike half of you. You wish you had my strength. You wouldn't blink if I was alive or dead. Come out my face.

Romeo and the audience share a long moment. They don't move. He doesn't want them to, not really. It's intimate. We want him to succeed even though he's pushing us away.

Romeo: *(To audience)* What?! Don't act like you care about what I do or how I end up. Stop sitting there waiting to see how this ends for me. You don't care. Go on, go.

The audience and the other three members of the company stay still, present.

A moment of something between the audience and the company. A breath. A reset. Something new.

*****

Romeo: *(To audience)* The waiting room is packed. These white kids banging out vocal warm-ups. It's got me bugging. I am hanging. I don't belong here. Why the hell am I here?

Romeo gets up to leave.

Panellist 1: Romeo Campbell?

Romeo: What!? Yeah, err yes that's me.

Panellist 1: Are you ready?

Romeo: Yeah. Yeah, I'm ready.

Panellist 1: Excellent. This way, please.

Romeo waits a beat. He could easily walk away. But doesn't.

The panellists settle themselves. Romeo stands there, nervously gathering himself, waiting to audition.

Panellist 3: In your own time, no rush.

The lights suddenly turn into a spotlight.

Romeo: *(His best attempt at a forced RP accent – like he thinks he's supposed to)* 'Tis torture and not mercy. Heaven is here, Where Juliet lives, and every cat and dog, And little mouse, Every unworthy thing, Live here in heaven and may look on her, But Romeo may not.

Panellist 2: Please stop.

Panellist 3: Why did you choose this speech?

Romeo: Erm… my name is Romeo?

Panellist 1: *(Encouraging)* Have you prepared any other speeches?

Romeo: Why would I do that?

Panellist 3: Why do you want to study here?

Romeo: I want to be an actor, innit.

Panellist 2: Then may I suggest you take some evening classes?

Romeo: Evening classes?

Panellist 3: They might be more suited to your background

Panellist 2: And current skill-set.

Romeo: But I wanna do this course.

Panellist 3: Perhaps you should gain some more life experience and audition in a few years?

Romeo: Bitch please, I've lived. Trust me, you don't even know the half of it.

Panellist 2: That kind of attitude and language has no place here.

Romeo: So I don't have no place here? Wow!

Panellist 3: Okay, thank you, next!

Romeo: I AIN'T FINISHED! You think I'm stupid, you think I'm some bottom-of-the-barrel bitch. You see this fucking finger right here? Take it and shove it up your arses.

Panellist 2: Please leave before I call security.

Romeo: Oh yeah, call security! *(With heavy sarcasm)* How about I do your jobs for you? SECURITY, SECURITY, SECURITY, SECURITY, there's a sexy black man in the building. Get him out NOWWWW!

Panellist 2: You are being extremely unprofessional.

Romeo: *(On the edge of tears. He's reached his limit)* I'm being myself!

Panellist 2: ...and you are proving my point.

Panellist 2 is smirking; Panellist 3 eyes Romeo nervously; but Panellist 1 has seen something in Romeo and is looking at him with interest.

Romeo: Fine, you don't want to see me now, you can pay premium to see me one day. You'll wish I came to your poxy little school.

Romeo feels frustrated. He tries to speak with composure but his emotions bleed through. The anger burns below to be replaced with only pain and determination.

Romeo: You think I wanted to come here and humiliate myself in front of you? You think I didn't walk past that front door ten times before I came in? That my hand weren't trembling when I typed in my application?

I knew you wouldn't get me.

I knew you wouldn't see or hear me.

You look at me and you see attitude and unprofessionalism.

You don't see me or anyone like me.

Cause we can't trust you with who we are.

But we are here.

I am here.

Romeo has a moment of realisation. He speaks with clarity, poise and power.

Romeo: I am a strong, talented, vulnerable, black gay man. I am gold dust. Right in front of you. Shaking. Hungry. Raw but ready. Fierce. I am here.

A beat.

No one speaks.

Romeo wipes his cheek, crosses over to his belongings and gathers them up. He knows he has given all he has.

As he begins to leave:

Panellist 1: *(With kindness and warmth)* Well, in that case we'd be fools to miss out. *(Getting up and approaching Romeo)* Shall we start again? With your own speech, this time?

Romeo: My own speech?

Panellist 1: I get the feeling that might be better?

Romeo: Better than Shakespeare?

Panellist 1: I'm sure Shakespeare won't mind the competition. Why don't you tell us some more about yourself? Why not act that out?

Romeo: You think you can handle it?

Panellist 1 gives Panellists 2 and 3 a look.

Panellist 3: *(Sighs)* Probably not.

Panellist 2: *(Smiles)* ...but why stop now?

Romeo: *(Smiles back)* Yeah.... why stop now?

Romeo thinks for a moment before he begins. In a repeat of the first moments of the play.

Romeo: It's 1998 on the Lightfoot Estate, North London. I'm five years old, sitting next to my big brother Perry, and Mum's painting our nails.

The music from the opening plays as the lights fade.

END

Also available from Team Angelica Publishing

Prose

'Reasons to Live' by Rikki Beadle-Blair
'What I Learned Today' by Rikki Beadle-Blair
'Faggamuffin' by John R Gordon
'Colour Scheme' by John R Gordon
'Souljah' by John R Gordon
'Drapetomania' by John R Gordon
'Hark' by John R Gordon
'Mother of Serpents' by John R Gordon
'Fairytales for Lost Children' by Diriye Osman
'Cuentos Para Niños Perdidos' – Spanish language edition of 'Fairytales For
          Lost Children', trans. Héctor F. Santiago
'The Butterfly Jungle' by Diriye Osman
'Black & Gay in the UK' ed. John R Gordon & Rikki Beadle-Blair
'Sista!' ed. Phyll Opoku-Gyimah, John R Gordon & Rikki Beadle-Blair
'More Than – the Person Behind the Label' ed. Gemma Van Praagh
'Tiny Pieces of Skull' by Roz Kaveney
'Fimí sílè Forever' by Nnanna Ikpo
'Lives of Great Men' by Chike Frankie Edozien
'Lord of the Senses' by Vikram Kolmannskog
'Movies That Made Me Gay' by Larry Duplechan

Playtexts

'Slap' by Alexis Gregory
'Custody' by Tom Wainwright
'#Hashtag Lightie' by Lynette Linton
'Summer in London' by Rikki Beadle-Blair
'I AM [NOT] KANYE WEST' by Natasha Brown
'Fierce' – a monologue anthology ed. Rikki Beadle-Blair
'Common' – a monologue anthology ed. Rikki Beadle-Blair
'Lit' – a monologue anthology ed. Rikki Beadle-Blair
'Bi-topia' by Sam Danson

Poetry

'Charred' by Andreena Leeanne
'Saturn Returns' by Sonny Nwachukwu
'Selected Poems 2009-2021' by Roz Kaveney
'The Great Good Time' by Roz Kaveney
'Perfect.Scar' by Robert Chevara